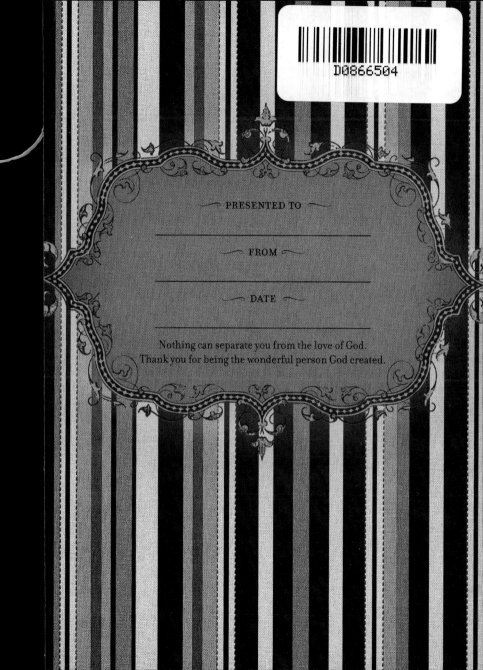

PRESENTED TO

FROM

DATE

Nothing can separate you from the love of God.
Thank you for being the wonderful person God created.

# PEARLS
## FROM
# HEAVEN
### Your Heavenly Father's
### Words of Love and Comfort

## mary grace birkhead

Design by Brand Navigation
Bill Chiaravalle, DeAnna Pierce,
Russ McIntosh & Brittany Gerwig

**INTEGRITY®**
PUBLISHERS
*Nashville*

THIS BOOK IS DEDICATED TO MY PARENTS,

# FRANK & JOAN PENNINGTON,

WHO LOVE ME WITH SUCH UNCONDITIONAL LOVE.

I LOVE YOU.

Thank you to my husband, Rob, who shares with me in the adventure of finding "pearls." To my dear children Robert, Daniel, and Camille, who are my "pearls of great price." To the people who remind me of who and whose I am: Trisha McDermott, Sarah Young, Melinda Seibert, Roseanne Coleman, Tiffany Foss, Mary Trapnell, Susan Lipson, Julie Ward, "The Fabulous 40" Bible study leaders, and my pastors, Lloyd Shadrach and Jeff Schulte. Also the brave people at Integrity Publishers for believing in these books: Byron Williamson, Mark Gilroy, Barb James, Betty Woodmancy, Dale Wilstermann, and Joey Paul. And special thanks to Bill Chiaravalle, DeAnna Pierce, Russ McIntosh, and Brittany Gerwig for making this book so beautiful.

# INTRODUCTION

 *Pearls are miracles.* They are made over time under very special conditions.

Pearls are precious. They are priced at a premium for their uniqueness.

Pearls are discoveries. They are embedded in a shell underwater waiting to be uncovered.

Pearls are rare. They are celebrated when they are found.

They don't form in groups like peas. And unlike diamonds, they are solitary–not hewn off something larger. They are individually unique.

Traditionally, they are the gift of choice from the bridegroom to his bride.

God's Word is filled with "pearls." He has them waiting for you. They are unique; each one has something very specific about you. His pearls for you are priceless; they contain all truth and all wisdom. He longs for you to have them, string them together, and wear them close. Gather them and adorn yourself with His power, His desire, His truth, His passionate love, His promises, His faithfulness, His unwavering acceptance—all for you!

Pearls become more lustrous and colorful the longer they are worn. Unlike many things of this world that wear out, pearls richen with age. The natural oil in your skin brings out the true quality of the pearl. So, the closer you wear them and the longer you hold them the more beauty they will reveal.

God's pearls—His promises found in the Bible—are just like that. The more time you spend meditating on them, the more they will bless you. Unlike what the world offers, God's truths are eternal, not temporary fixes. His Words are refreshing and filled with life. God's Word is full of pearls; would you like to try on a strand?

YOU ARE
**HIS CHILD**
HEBREWS 2:11-13

*You are a child of the King.*

You are His beloved daughter.

He wants you to be in His presence.

He calls to you.

Bring all your hopes, longings, sorrows, and

cares and lay them at His feet.

You are welcome in the throne room!

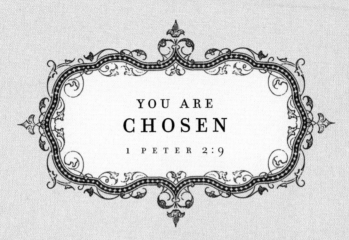

YOU ARE
**CHOSEN**
1 PETER 2:9

*You are called out of darkness into His marvelous light.*

You show forth His praises.

He lives in you and shines out of you.

You are filled with His power and light.

You are no longer a slave,

but an heir of the King!

Hallelujah!

YOU WILL BE
## FILLED
JEREMIAH 31:14

*Your soul will be satisfied*
*with God's goodness.*

He will sustain you, no matter the situation.

He will pour into you as you are poured out.

You won't run empty.

Don't trust in your strength, trust His.

There is no end to His goodness!

## YOU CAN
## REST

P S A L M 55:22

*You don't need to carry a burden.*

He wants you to have a light load.

Take every thought captive.

Hold each worry up to His light.

He is able to lift the weight off you.

Cast your cares on Him. He cares for you.

So unpack your heavy bags and rest!

YOU HAVE
**HOPE**
ISAIAH 40:31

*You are becoming strong*
*as you wait on the Lord.*

He will give you the strength to hold on.

He is not weak. He won't let you fall.

He will provide your foot with

a firm place to stand.

He won't be late. He is trustworthy.

Help is on the way!

YOUR SORROW WILL
**BECOME JOY**
2 THESSALONIANS 2:16-17

## *You will be comforted on sad days.*

God will console your heart. He can give

you what you need for the moment.

He is able to redeem what has been

taken away. He sees your tears and sadness.

He desires to turn your sorrow into joy!

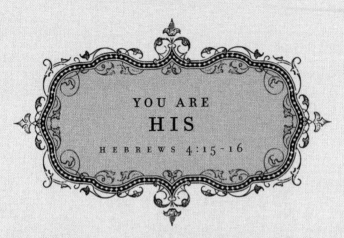

YOU ARE
**HIS**
HEBREWS 4:15-16

*You have a God that knows*
*all your weaknesses and needs.*

He's walked in your shoes. He knows it's
hard! He delights to show you mercy
and give you grace. He has compassion on
you and sees your heart.
Your need is not looked down on by Him.
You are His beloved child.

YOU WILL BE
## REWARDED
HEBREWS 11:6

*Your faith pleases God.*

He enjoys your trust in Him.

Your prayers are heard.

Your courage brings Him honor.

He sees your small, unseen sacrifices.

You're doing a great job. Keep trusting!

YOU WILL BE

## SATISFIED

PSALM 63:3-5

*Your spirit will be supplied*
*with good things.*

His loving kindness is better than life.

He is the Giver of all good things.

He serves you from His banquet table.

What He provides is eternal

and perfect for you.

Praise Him with joyful lips!

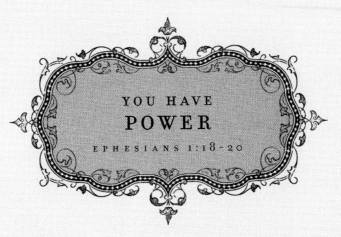

YOU HAVE
**POWER**
EPHESIANS 1:18-20

*You are equipped with all
you need today.*

God has gone out before you.

You are secure in His protection.

You won't be left with nothing.

God gives out of His abundance.

God is never surprised!

YOU ARE
**CARED FOR**
ISAIAH 58:11

*You are a well-watered garden.*

God keeps watch over you.

Turn your face to His beautiful light.

He will continue to pour life into you.

Your dry soil can

be saturated with His lavish Spirit.

Bask in the warmth

of His immeasurable grace.

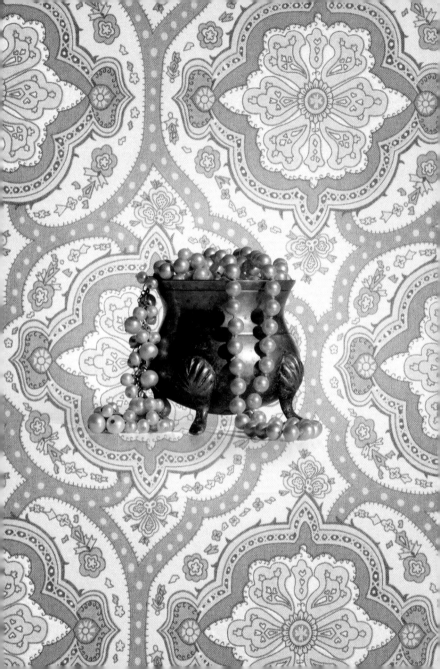

YOU WILL BE
## COMFORTED
PHILIPPIANS 4:6-7

# *You don't have to be anxious.*

God will give you peace.

He is a God of details.

He will surround you with comfort.

His all-seeing Spirit is actively working

on your behalf.

Pray and receive what He has for you!

YOU ARE
**HEAD**
PSALM 40:1-3

*Your prayers are heard by God.*

Your prayer is an act of faith.

Nothing is impossible with Him.

He will rescue you and

put you on firm ground.

Your life will be a song to Him.

The world will be amazed at God!

YOU ARE
**KNOWN**
MATTHEW 10:30

*Your Father knows you
inside and out.*

He made you with His holy hands.

He embraces all of you—your "good"

and your "bad." He's been with you every

moment of your life.

Every hair is numbered.

They might be a mess, but they're numbered!

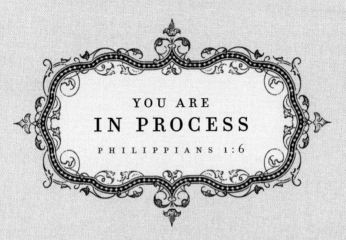

YOU ARE
**IN PROCESS**
PHILIPPIANS 1:6

*You are becoming perfected
in Christ.*

He's been working in you.

He will continue to mold and shape you.

The frustrations in your life

are His sandpaper.

Hold still and let Him do His job.

He knows exactly what He's doing.

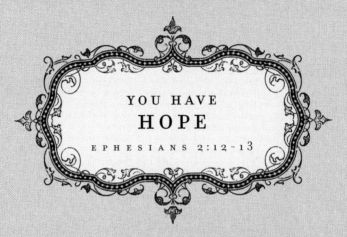

YOU HAVE
## HOPE
EPHESIANS 2:12-13

*You have been bought
with a price.*

You are worth more than gold.

He sees you as His precious child.

Pray that He will open your eyes to that fact.

No good thing will He withhold from you.

Jesus made it all possible!

**YOU ARE**
## RESCUED
2 SAMUEL 22:17-20

*Your needs are not too much for God.*

He holds all the earth in His control.

He sustains all of life.

It is not a frustration or a difficulty for Him

to care for you.

He will give to you in abundance.

He wants to provide for you!

YOU HAVE BEEN
## ADOPTED
ROMANS 8:15-17

## *You have not been abandoned.*

God has adopted you.

You, who were far away,

have been brought near.

He delights in the fact that you are His.

Yes, life is hard. And yes, you are His child!

He is your Daddy, Papa, Abba!

YOU ARE
**SAFE**

PSALM 4:8

*You are blessed and restored as you sleep.*

He is carefully watching over you.

Rest in the fact that

His eyes are always on you.

Fall asleep knowing

He is restoring you in every way.

Sweet dreams!

YOU ARE
**FREE**

ROMANS 8:1-2

*You don't have to carry a*
*burden of shame.*

With God there is no condemnation.

You have been declared "not guilty."

Christ's righteousness is now yours.

He's the lifter of your head.

The chains of shame are cut. Now fly!

YOU ARE
**NEW**

2 CORINTHIANS 5:17

*You are a new creation.*

The old you is dying away.

The power of the Holy Spirit is your defense.

He is breaking the bonds of your past.

He's redeeming the years you've lost.

You are looking

more like your Father everyday!

YOU ARE
## HIS TREASURE
DEUTERONOMY 26:18-19

*You are precious.*

You are a pearl of great price.

You have been declared righteous.

God paid a big price for you

and delights in your devotion to Him.

Your worth is beyond measure!

YOU ARE
**PROTECTED**
PSALM 34:7

*You are not alone.*

He is next to you right now!

And He is always there

no matter where you go or what you do.

He continually offers you great hope!

Release all your worries and fears to Him.

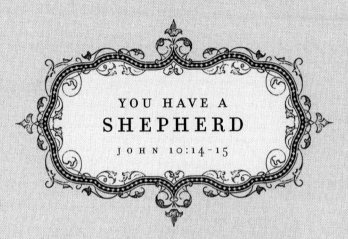

## YOU HAVE A
## SHEPHERD
JOHN 10:14-15

*You are His sheep.*

He's watching out for you.

He knows your tendency to wander.

Listen for His voice; He's calling to you.

Follow Him to the greenest grass.

You will be most satisfied in His presence.

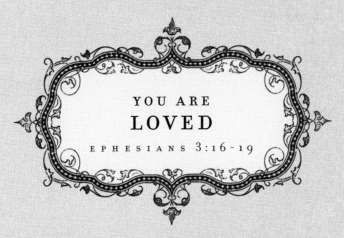

YOU ARE
LOVED
EPHESIANS 3:16-19

*You are being strengthened*
*in your innermost being.*

You are being rooted and established in love.

He is revealing His great love to you and for

you. He is transforming your mind

as you turn your thoughts to Him. You are given

great hope and power as you trust in Him. Let

the wind blow; you are firmly planted!

YOU NEED
GOD
ISAIAH 55:8-9

*Your thoughts are not His thoughts.*

Give your expectations of others and

your circumstances over to Him.

Let Him orchestrate all the details.

His plans may not be your plans,

but He sees the big picture.

He knows the end of the story.

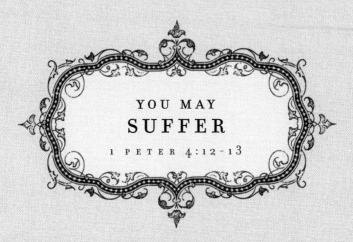

YOU MAY
**SUFFER**
1 PETER 4:12-13

*You are becoming like Him.*

He is glorified as you focus on Him.

Your sufferings can bring Him glory.

He has experienced life like this too.

Especially in the hard times, He can shine

through you.

That's a painful, yet beautiful, truth!

YOU KNOW
**THE KING**

1 TIMOTHY 1:17

## *You can rest today.*

He has it all under control.

You can give Him your "to-do" list.

He holds all time in His hands.

He is powerful and over all things.

Enjoy each moment.

The King is on His throne.

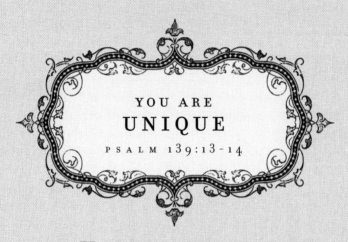

YOU ARE

**UNIQUE**

PSALM 139:13-14

*You are unique.*

He made you very special.

You are not a mistake or a second thought.

You were planned by God.

Nothing was left out.

He delights in His creation of you.

Let Him see that big smile!

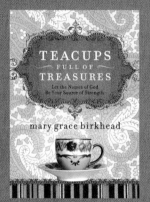